MINISTRY OF MUNITIONS.

Technical Department - Aircraft Production.

I.C.—627.

July, 1918.

Report on the
2-Seater Rumpler, G 117

The Naval & Military Press Ltd

Published by
The Naval & Military Press Ltd
5 Riverside, Brambleside, Bellbrook
Industrial Estate, Uckfield, East Sussex,
TN22 1QQ England

Tel: +44 (0) 1825 749494
Fax: +44 (0) 1825 765701

www.naval-military-press.com
www.military-genealogy.com

In reprinting in facsimile from the original, any imperfections are inevitably reproduced and the quality may fall short of modern type and cartographic standards.

MINISTRY OF MUNITIONS.

Technical Department - Aircraft Production.

I.C.—627.   July, 1918.

Report on the
2-Seater Rumpler, G 117

REPORT

ON

Two-Seater Rumpler Biplane, G.117

(260 H.P. MERCEDES ENGINE).

This machine, which was used by the enemy at the commencement of the year, is of the CV type but differs only in detail from the earlier CIV type.

The general shape and disposition of the wings is maintained, including the characteristic sweep-back of the main planes, and the fitting of ailerons to the upper planes only. Some important particulars follow:—

Weight empty (but with water)	2439 lbs.
Weight, fully loaded	3439 lbs.
Total military load	545 lbs.
Area of upper wings (with ailerons)	217.6 sq. ft.
Area of lower wings	146 sq. ft.
Total area of main planes	363.6 sq. ft.
Loading per sq. ft. of wing surface	9.5 lbs.
Area of tail plane	22 sq. ft.
Area of fin	4 sq. ft.
Area of elevators	20.8 sq. ft.
Area of rudder	6 sq. ft.
Total weight per H.P.	13.2 lbs.
Petrol capacity	59 gallons.
Oil capacity	3 gallons.
Water capacity	10 gallons.
Endurance	About 4 hours.

PERFORMANCE.

	ft.	m.p.h.	revs.
Speed at	10,000	100.5	1510
Speed at	15,000	87	1390

	ft.	m. s.	Rate of climb in ft. per min.	revs.
Climb to	10,000	16 0	400	1375
Climb to	15,000			

Service ceiling, 15,500 ft. (estimated).
Estimated absolute ceiling, 17,500 ft.
Greatest height reached, 15,300 ft. in 38 min. 25 secs. Rate of climb at this height is 125 ft. per min.

CONTROL.

Longitudinal (elevators), good.
Lateral (ailerons), very heavy and very ineffective.
Directional (rudder), moderately light and quite effective.

It is reported that the machine is tiring to fly owing to the very poor lateral control; that it is nose-heavy, and rather liable to get into a spin.

WINGS.

The upper wings have a maximum span of 41 ft. 6 in., and a chord of 5 ft. 8 in. The span of the lower wings is 40 ft., and the chord is 4 ft. 4 in.

The wings are swept back through an angle of 3 deg., and are set at 2½ deg. dihedral angle. The wing sections of upper and lower planes are given in Fig. 1. Both front and rear spars are of spruce, and are constructed in two halves, which are grooved and

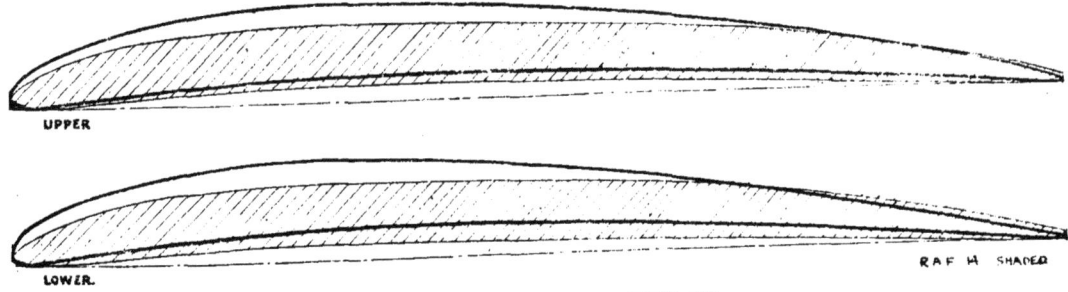

SECTION OF AEROFOIL — RUMPLER C.V.
R.A.F 14 SECTION SUPERIMPOSED.

tongued, and then glued together. This is clearly indicated in Fig. 2. The ribs are built up of ply wood and strips in the usual manner, and are of good workmanship. Short ribs join the front spar to the leading edge, alternately with the true ribs.

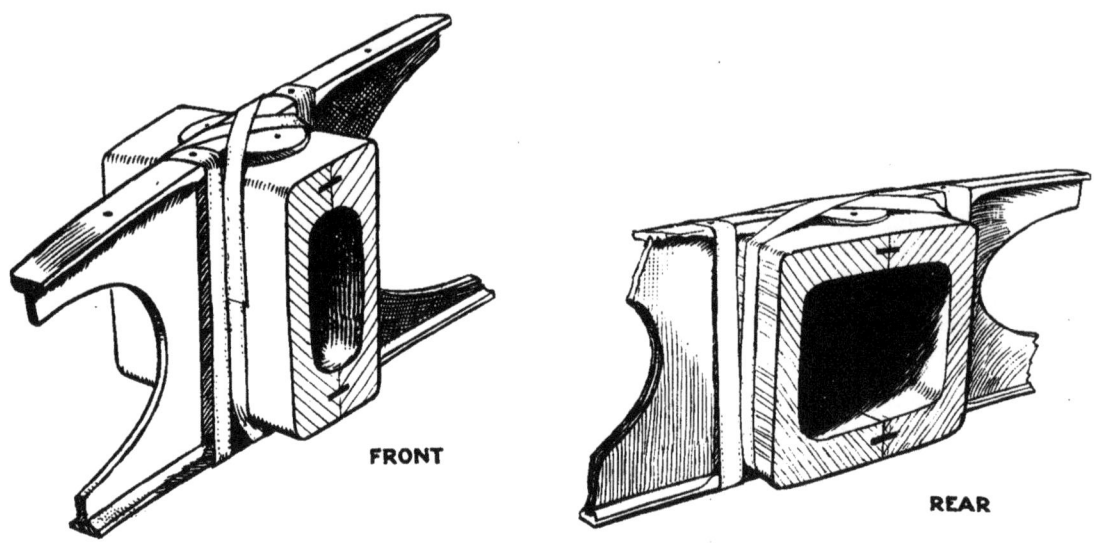

Fig. 2.

The wing construction appears adequately strong. Steel compression tubes are placed between the spars, and are braced by ties varying from piano wire at the wing tips to cable and swaged rod at the inner end. The trailing edge consists of a flattened steel tube, to which the ribs are attached by copper rivets.

Ailerons are fitted to the upper wing only, which may in some measure account for that ineffectiveness of lateral control which is characteristic of nearly all German aeroplanes. The area of each aileron is 15.3 sq. ft.

The methods of attaching the main planes to the upper cabane and to the fuselage are designed to assist rapidity of assembly and dis-assembly, and are of considerable interest. They do not differ from the arrangement on CIV machines, and may be considered, therefore, to have been found satisfactory in practice. From the Fig. 3 it will be seen that the upper wings are locked by means of a guillotine lever, held in position by a pin passing through both levers and through two holes arranged in the centre section. The lower wings are locked in position by even simpler means (Fig. 4), requiring no moving parts. The ball at the end of the spar is simply introduced into the socket fixed to the fuselage, and the wing tip is kept lowered. When the tip is raised, the top portion of the wing attachment slips into position, thus locking the wing in such a manner that, even before the attachment of struts and bracing, movement is possible in only one way—i.e., by the dropping of the wing tip. A label bearing instructions and an explanatory diagram referring to these lower wing attachments is affixed on either side of the fuselage, near to the socket concerned.

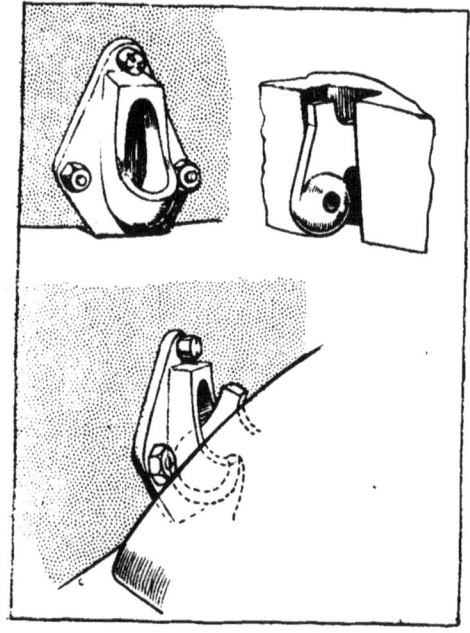
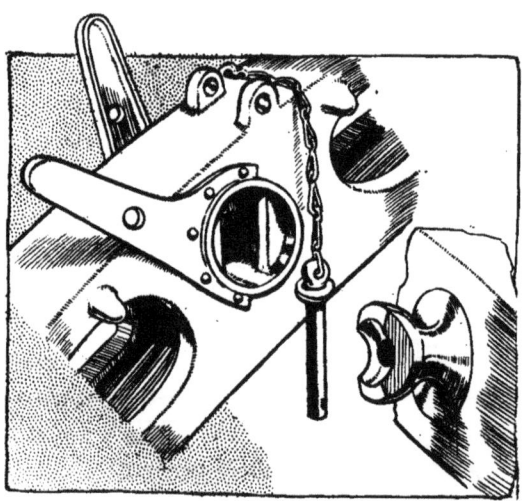

Fig. 3. Fig. 4.

STRUTS.

These are of circular section steel tube, encased in a wood fairing. A typical Rumpler strut attachment is shown in Fig. 5. The twin sockets are held down by two bolts, which pass right through the spars. The heads of these bolts are clearly shown.

Fig. 5.

The construction of the welded-up centre section cabane may be gathered from the photographs and from Fig. 6.

A cylindrical well of 3-ply and aluminium is incorporated in the lower wing close to the fuselage on the left side to accommodate the compass, which is thus convenient to the pilot's sight. Fig. 7 shows the construction of this well.

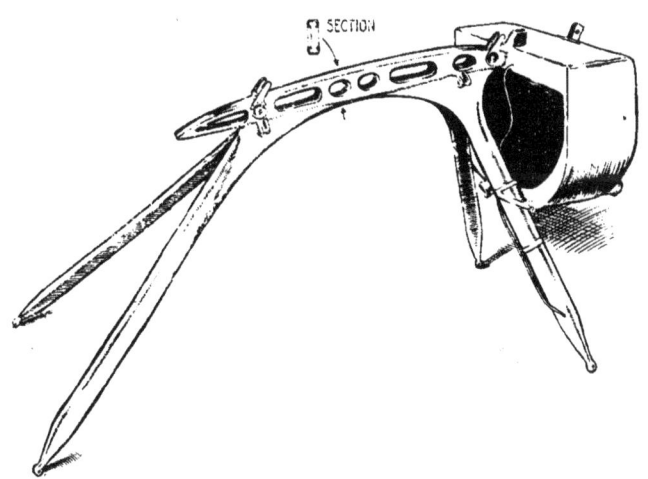

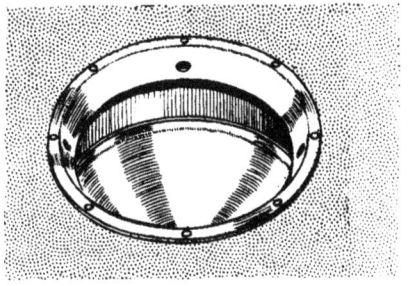

Fig. 6.

Fig. 7.

FUSELAGE.

The fuselage is a compromise between the several rival methods of construction. Wooden longerons and struts, braced with piano wire; steel tubes, and 3-ply are all used in varying degrees.

A braced girder of longerons and cross struts constitutes the principal factor, and this construction is depended upon entirely in the rear of the observer's cockpit. Towards the tail, for a distance of about 6 ft. from the sternpost, the covering is of 3-ply, which thoroughly stiffens up the fuselage where the stresses due to the tailplanes may be most severely felt. The middle portion of the fuselage sides—i.e., between the 3-ply at the rear and the pilot's seat, has fabric covering, while forward of this 3-ply is again used.

The slightly arched top fairing is entirely of 3-ply, except for the aluminium cowl, which extends to the rear of the gunner's cockpit, as also is the bottom of the fuselage. The engine cowls are of aluminium, held in place by turnbuttons. From the rear of the observer's cockpit to the front of the pilot's seat the wood construction is reinforced by steel tubes, which have forked ends, and are bolted together.

The pilot's cockpit is particularly roomy and comfortably fitted. The gunner is provided with a seat of the piano-stool type with a rotatable head. This head is fixed on its shaft eccentrically, as may be seen by Fig. 8.

Fig. 8.

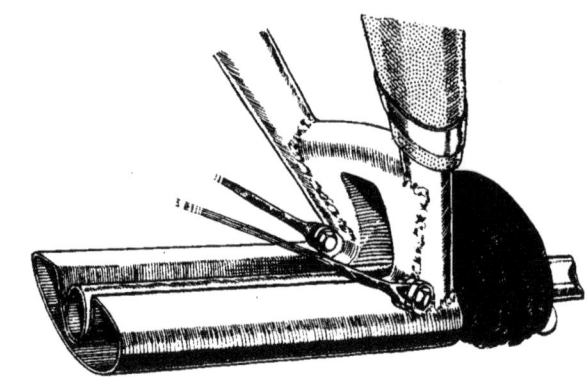

Fig. 9.

LANDING GEAR.

The undercarriage, of the usual vee type, while presenting few noteworthy features, is of workmanlike design and construction.

Both front and rear limbs are of stream-line section steel tubing. The upper extremities are placed well apart. At the lower extremities the tubes are welded together to form, together with the sheet steel axle fairing, the slot to accommodate axle travel. (See Fig. 9.) The front limb, which is of smaller section than the rear tube, is additionally faired with wood, while the rear limb is naked. The wood fairing has obviously been fitted as an afterthought, and not by the manufacturer. The job is clumsy and without finish, though effective. Landing shocks are taken by the familiar steel coil spring.

Four bracing wires are employed, connecting all four upper attachment points to the apices of the vees. Fig. 10 shows one of the front joints.

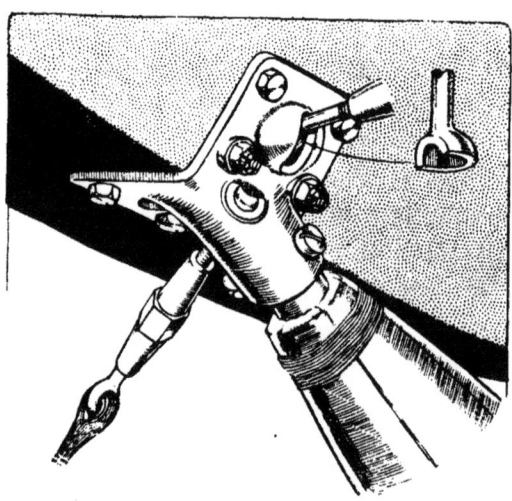

Fig. 10.

TAIL.

The tail is practically of standard Rumpler—and, indeed, German—practice, but it is noteworthy that the elevators, which were of the balanced pattern in the CIV machine, are no longer so. As the longitudinal control is reported entirely satisfactory, it is evident that unbalanced elevators have been found all that is desired. The fin may hardly be regarded as adequate, in view of the side area presented in the nose of the machine, and the report that this aeroplane is somewhat liable to spin should be considered in this connection.

The four tail stays are of stream-line steel tube, and the lower pair have serrated edges to assist mechanics in remembering that these stays should not be grasped in lifting the machine or in holding it back on starting.

Although the fabric has not been removed, these members—the fin, rudder, and elevators—appear to be constructed of light steel tube welded in the usual way.

The tail skid is of ash, pivoted in the centre, and sprung at its upper end. The lower end carries a sheet steel shoe, whose shape is shown in Fig. 11.

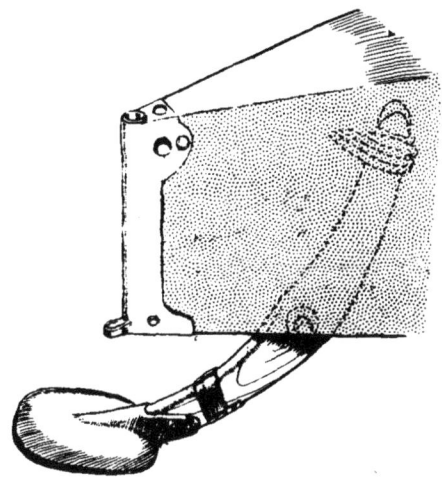

Fig. 11.

CONTROLS.

The control system is of considerable interest, inasmuch as the usual transverse rocking shaft operating the elevator controls is not used. The aileron control is actuated by a longitudinal rocking shaft of steel tube, which carries a welded cone-shaped portion supporting the vertical control lever. The aileron cables are attached to a lever pinned to the rocking shaft, and pass through the wings, operating the ailerons in the way that has become usual in German aeroplanes—i.e., the aileron lever lies in line with the plane, and is accommodated in a slot cut in the rear edge of the main plane.

The control cables pass over pulleys when they leave the lower plane to be attached to the aileron lever. These pulleys are situated behind the rear outer strut attachment, and are capped with a neat aluminium fairing.

The control lever operates the cables attached to the elevator levers, those attached to the lower extremities of the levers passing over pulleys mounted in the front portion of the rocking shaft. This shaft projects somewhat below the level of the fuselage bottom, and is neatly faired off by an aluminium shield screwed to the fuselage. The control system should be made clear by Fig. 12.

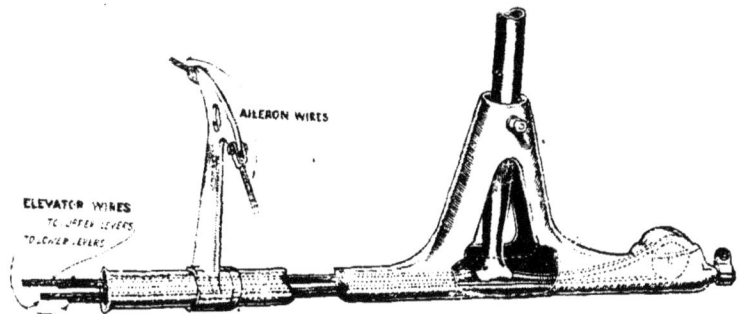

Fig. 12.

A welded sheet steel rudder bar of simple pattern, shown in Fig. 13, operates the rudder through the usual cables. The distance between the seat and rudder bar is not variable. Rubber sleeves and leather straps on either extremity guard against the possibility of the pilot's feet slipping.

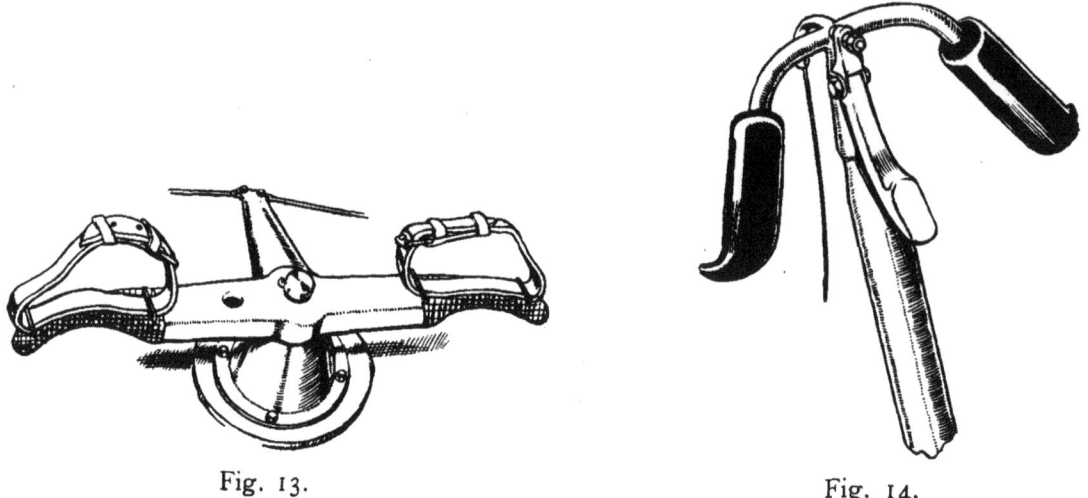

Fig. 13.   Fig. 14.

ARMAMENT.

The pilot controls the fire of one fixed Spandau gun attached close to starboard side of the engine. The cocking lever is placed just outside the cockpit to the pilot's right. The gun itself is inaccessible during flight. A thumb lever shown in sketch (14) controls the fire through the usual clutch and synchronising gear.

The observer's gun is of the Parabellum type; and is mounted on the usual built-up wooden gun-ring, of the same kind as that found on most German machines.

Provision for the fitting of a bomb rack had been made, but none was fitted.

An aluminium tray with holes for 10 Verey lights was fixed to the fuselage.

ENGINE.

The Rumpler is usually fitted with a 240 H.P. Maybach engine or a 260 H.P. Mercedes. The present example has 6 cylinder Mercedes of 260 H.P., which possesses the familiar combined throttle and altitude control. The exhaust gases are led into a welded manifold, the shape of which is indicated in the photograph.

COOLING SYSTEM.

The radiator, made by Hans Windhoff, is slung over the rear portion of the engine, and fixed to the central cabane. The honeycomb consists of circular brass tubes, expanded at their extremities into hexagons, and sweated together there. The total radiating surface is approximately 1.5 sq. ft. The shutters which regulate the cooling surface are shown in Fig. 15. They are operated by cables passing over pulleys. One cable passes over the top of the radiator, while the other exerts a downward pull and passes underneath. German pilots have reported that these shutters are rarely required except during protracted descents.

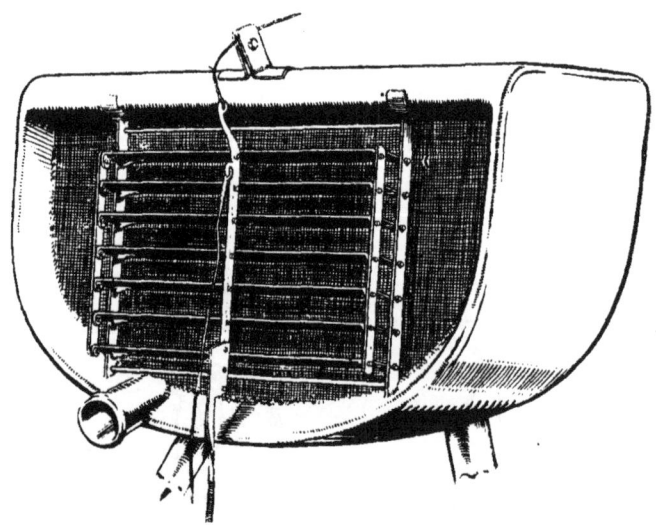

Fig. 15.

The temperature of the water is indicated by a mercury thermometer easily visible from the pilot's seat, and the limits of the permissible range of temperature are defined by red marks—one at 60 deg. and the other at 85 deg. The radiator may be considered thoroughly satisfactory, but must naturally obstruct the pilot's view to some extent.

The oil tank is situated at the port side of the engine, and the maintenance of an equable temperature of its contents is assisted by a thick covering of felt. The oil pump is embedded in the bottom of the crank case, and not only passes on the oil to the gudgeon pins and crankshaft, but at the same time mixes, at each pulsation, a certain quantity of fresh oil from the tank with the oil already in circulation.

PETROL SYSTEM.

The main petrol tank—of 46 gallons capacity—serves as a support for the pilot's seat, while an auxiliary tank holding 13 gallons is fitted between the two cockpits, adapting itself to the shape of the fuselage top fairing and to the gunner's turret. Neither tank seems to possess baffle plates, and both work under pressure.

The initial pressure is obtained by means of hand pumps, of which there is one in each of the cockpits. An automatic air pressure pump driven off the crankshaft maintains the pressure, and a release valve incorporated in the pump regulates it. Each tank has its own pressure gauge on the dashboard. The petrol gauge on the main tank is of Laufer make, while a Maximall gauge is found on the auxiliary tank. All pipes on this machine are of copper, and the tanks of sheet brass.

ENGINE CONTROLS.

Three 3-way cocks are fitted. They enable the pilot to shut off the petrol entirely; to supply from both tanks simultaneously, or to run on either of the tanks alone.

The throttle controls are shown in Fig. 16. The placing of the Mercedes carburettor at the rear of the engine facilitates the direct nature of the control.

The Deuta tachometer, working on the centrifugal principle, is driven off the camshaft, and is graduated from 0 to 1600 R.P.M. It is not illuminated, and no normal is marked.

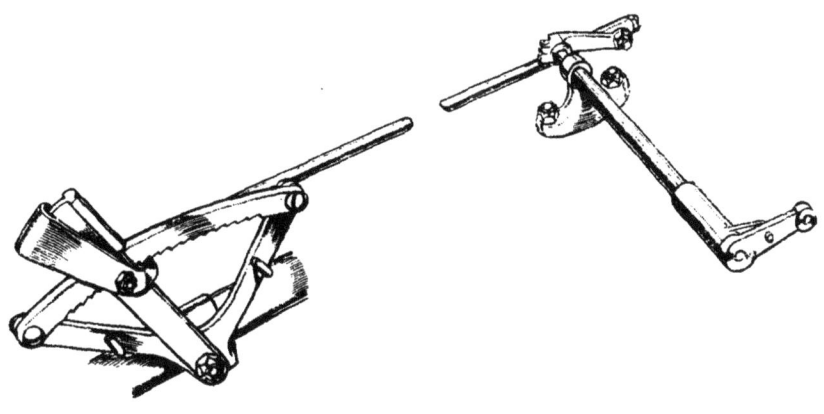

Fig. 16.

PROPELLER.

The propeller is an "Axial," No. 6987. diameter 3150 mm., pitch 1830 mm. It is secured to the crankshaft by eight bolts, an extra pair being fitted between two of the pairs of the usual six.

WIRELESS.

The machine is internally wired, and a tapping key is fitted to the gunner's right hand. The rack intended to support the aerial reel is also to be found, as well as a sheet steel dynamo shelf near the engine.

CAMERAS.

Two types of cameras were fitted. One particularly large one was accommodated in the special fitting shown in Fig. 17. The light octagonal tray A is suspended from the floor boards by elastic shock absorbers.

The zinc well shown in Fig. 18 carried the second camera. A light ply-wood tube, 30 in. long and 5 in. wide, is fixed to the rear of the observer's seat. It is obviously intended to carry some object, probably a Goerz bombing sight.

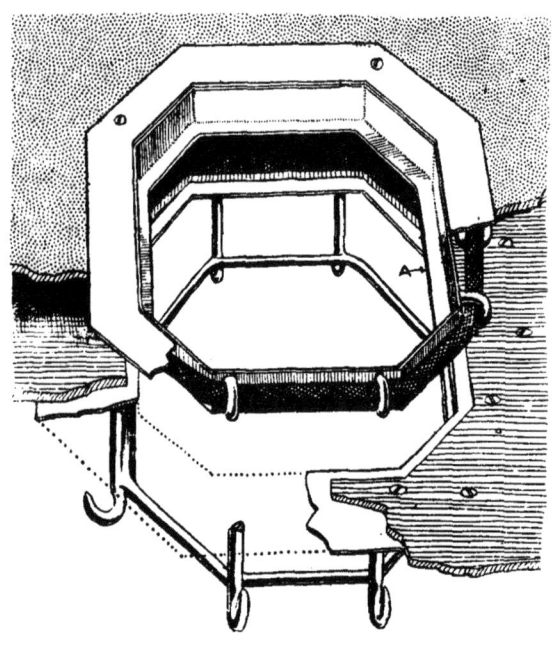

Fig. 17.

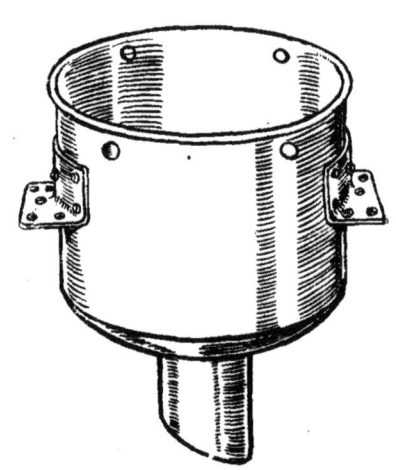

Fig. 18.

This machine is now at the Enemy Aircraft View Room, Agricultural Hall, Islington, where it may be seen on production of a pass, obtainable from The Controller, Technical Dept., Ap.D.(L), Pen Corner House, Kingsway, W.C. 2.

G. T. C.,

Ap.D.(L).

J. G. WEIR,

Brigadier-General,

Controller, Technical Department.

Front View.

Rear View.

Three-quarter Rear View.

The Exhaust Manifold and Engine Cowling.

The Radiator and Connections.

View of the Tail.

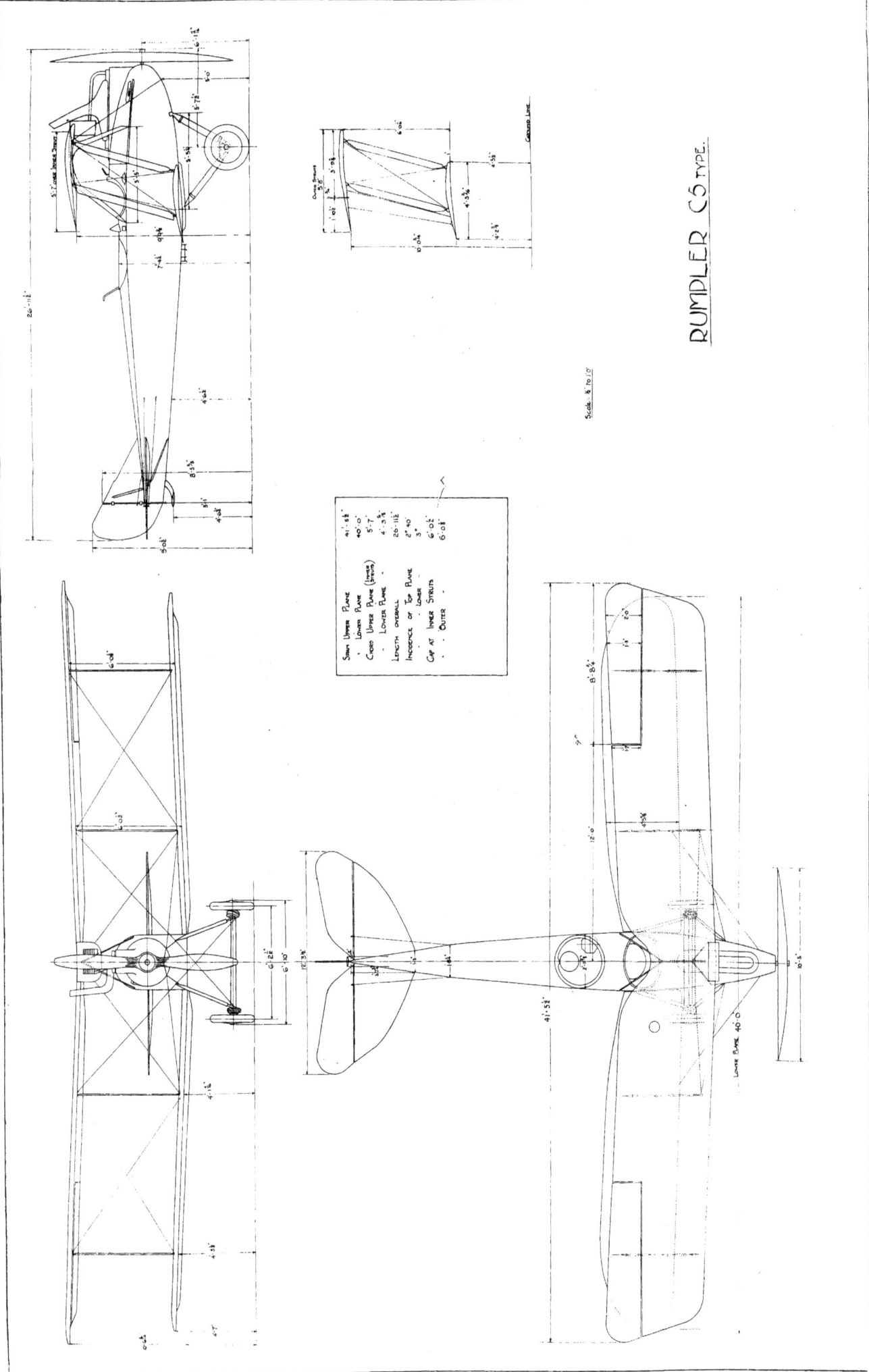

www.ingramcontent.com/pod-product-compliance
Ingram Content Group UK Ltd.
Pitfield, Milton Keynes, MK11 3LW, UK
UKHW051526180426
11947UKWH00019B/1591